Online Dating is Hell
(and Hella Hilarious)

Online Dating is Hell (and Hella Hilarious)

A Real Woman's Real Conversations with Real Men Online

by
Tinder Hella

Hella Good House of Publishing

Copyright © 2018 by TinderHella

All rights reserved. No part of this book may be reproduced in any form or by any electronic or mechanical means including information storage and retrieval systems, without permission in writing from the author. The only exception is by a reviewer, who may quote short excerpts in a review.

Cover designed by Angie Alaya (pro_eboookcovers)

This book is a work of non-fiction. Names and locations have been changed to protect the guilty and the innocent

HellaMean.com

TinderHella.com

Printed in the United States of America

First Printing: January 2018

Hella Good House of Publishing

ISBN-13: 978-0-9996819-4-7

ISBN-10: 0-9996819-4-7

For DTD

I used it for words.

Thank You

R - Whether or not you take the blame...I mean credit...I will always attribute it to you

E & E

PI, IWALYNMW

My inner circle of friends who will exist in my life always (PS, DC, MJ, ZP, TR, L, 7, to name but a few)

The Triple Goddesses - KC, PR, DD - Thank you, bitches.

SB

Everyone who showed me redemption is possible

Every single person who went up against TinderHella and lived to tell the tale

ONLINE DATING IS HELL

TABLE OF CONTENTS

Prologue 1

In the Beginning... 5

Tinder Godmother 9

Simple Lines for Simple Minds 13

"Small" Talk 21

Desperation - A New Cologne for Men 25

Block Heads 29

Jackson 33

Profiles 45

Thanksgiving 47

Christmas 49

New Year's Eve 57

You Little Devil 61

Hockey 67

Zach 75

Star Wars 83

ONLINE DATING IS HELL

OKCupid 85
Q&A 87
The Email Where I Have Officially Been Deemed Attractive 93
I Didn't See That Coming 95
Hella - the Reboot 103
Harry Potter 105
Game Night at Hella's House 107
I Am That Friend 111
Epilogue 113
About TinderHella 115

ONLINE DATING IS HELL

PROLOGUE

I had been married for 16 and a half years when I separated from my ex-husband. Looking to jump start my sex life, I joined Tinder on Valentine's Day 2015 and took it seriously for about a whopping 15 minutes.

I tried to be shallow and just go for the good-looking dudes but too often the pretty boys were mentally lacking and dull as dirt. Turns out I needed some sort of mental stimulation to get beyond the phone screen.

GASP

I am pretty, so I was popular and met a lot of people and I am still friends with a few of my very early matches. Tinder has actually been very good to me, and a series of matches turned my entire life around, opening up a whole new world.

But before that I discovered a few things...

1) Guys will let a pretty girl get away with almost anything.
2) I'm hilarious.

If you think I'm a bitch, you are correct. I've been called a mean girl by a few men because my sense of humor can be harsh and not everyone's cup of tea. That being said I was never interested in collecting anyone's personal information, outing them to family and friends, or hurting them physically. I am not publishing anyone's pictures here, even though some of them made me laugh until I couldn't breathe.

ONLINE DATING IS HELL

I'll add a few comments here and there, more background details, and sometimes just my thoughts, but most of these exchanges stand on their own.

I wanted to keep in all typos and grammatical errors, but it was driving my editors crazy so unless it shows a repeated inability to follow the basic English language, the errors were corrected. I had to call in some ex-CIA and FBI cryptographers to decipher a few of these messages. Most of them quit. Some of you really need to get some help 'lerning werds'.

Names have been changed to protect the innocent, the guilty, and the douchebags. I'm very guilty so my name has been changed as well.

You're welcome.

ONLINE DATING IS HELL

Omg. That's hilarious. You have to do something with those.

> I wish
> I have a shitton

They're amazingly funny

> Now you're just trying to get into my pants

Nope I'm not playing that game. I've seen what you do to guys who take that bait

> You took the bait a long time ago, doll face

ONLINE DATING IS HELL

IN THE BEGINNING...

I didn't always keep track of my interactions. I laughed plenty but didn't feel the need to document these conversations.

Until Adam.

Adam was 30, which was the youngest I would even consider at the time. He seemed so overly excited in text that I had pictured him as a puppy dog, jumping up on every visitor who came to his home.

When we had decided to meet, he told me it would have to be close to his place because he didn't have a car. He explained that his financial situation was less than ideal and that bothered me. The day before our date, I cancelled.

Sunday he texted me

> Be honest with me. You cancelled because of me.

I decided to be painfully honest. I gave him a well thought out reply explaining that a man in his 30s not financially responsible enough to own a car bothered me and being 38 I didn't have to date someone like that. I also suggested that he not disclose that information next time. Take an Uber. Borrow a friend's car. I told him that girls didn't need to know anything even remotely about his finances this early. I really wish I had my message. It was tough love without sarcasm. I didn't expect to

ONLINE DATING IS HELL

get a reply so I deleted all of our text messages in my phone. But he did reply.

> Thanks for being so upfront and honest like a grownup
>
> Here's hoping whatever car owner you settle for next is worst than your last ex
>
> Cunt

I was so stunned, I could only reply with an emoji.

He surprisingly didn't stop there.

> If I was rich and had a place and a car your mouth and legs are wide open and that's not at all shallow to you.
>
> No wonder you're single at 38.
>
> Mouthy bitch indeed.

I knew just retelling the story would never do it justice. People needed to see it themselves, so I took a screenshot. Since I also knew there would be many more ridiculous conversations in the future, I decided to screenshot everything.

And so TinderHella was born.

ONLINE DATING IS HELL

Holy shit you are sexy as fuck. My name is Justin.

Are you even a real profile?

> I don't know. Are any of us real? Or are we just figments of someone's imagination? Brain chemistry is fascinating and sometimes even the slightest chemical imbalance can completely alter the body's perception of reality.

Lol...Epic response...I am even more intrigued. What's your name?

> TinderHella - you can call me Tinder

So what brings you to Tinder?

> Loneliness. Desperation. Self-hatred. Ya know, girl stuff.

Besides TinderHella, what can I call you?

> That Hot Chick Over There

Is tinderhella the opposite of tinderella?

> If Tinderella was the dream, I am the nightmare.

ONLINE DATING IS HELL

TINDER GODMOTHER

These guys are lucky I do pro bono work.

Hi. I'm your Tinder Godmother and I'm here to let you know you should use the 4th picture as your first and dump the one you currently have. The blue eyes will catch a lot more women.

You're welcome.

Good evening Billy-Bob, hope your Saturday is going so well you won't see this message until morning 😜

Just thought I would let you know that I really think the second picture in your profile should be the first picture. The picture of you holding the camera in front of the mirror isn't all that flattering. You should delete that one.

-signed your tinder godmother

ONLINE DATING IS HELL

Damn, don't even know how to begin. Refreshing to see your awesome metaphors after seeing so many "I like long walks on the beach and 'don't like games.'" I, on the other hand, love playing games. ;-) Anyway, nice to "meet" you!

> Games can be a lot of fun. I obviously don't take this app seriously
>
> A few tips for you: Exaggerate all your measurements (except weight - keep that low). Pick a hobby from the following: crossfit, hunting, fishing, traveling, excessive nerdism. Take a lot of obnoxious pictures of you doing said hobby. Say you cook, drink whiskey, and that basic bitches can swipe left.
>
> Bonus points for trying to dissuade crazy girls

Should I rent a fancy car, take some pics in it and pass it off as my own? I think I'm getting the hang of it.

> Exactly. Say you are looking for a partner in crime!
>
> You should be messaging me way more, btw. Several times in a row and then get angry when I don't reply after 15 minutes
>
> Why should you expect me to have a job, or a life, or some sense of self respect?

That's a good point. Totally my bad... Maybe I should take some time off so I can literally spend every waking moment staring at my phone? MAN I've got a lot to learn!

> Consider me your tinder godmother.

ONLINE DATING IS HELL

> Did all your female friends get together and tell you that hair was sexy? If so, you got punked.

Haha that's not hat hair. My hair is just curls when it gets long enough!

My hair's not like that now lol

> I'm here to be blunt. That picture needs to either be deleted or relegated to the back. Consider me your Tinder-godmother.

His profile: I ain't first class but I'm not white trash, I'm wild and a little crazy too. Some girls don't like boys like me but some girls do!

> Probability states that all outcomes added together will always equal 1, so if 7/12 of the girls don't like boys like you, it only makes sense that 5/12 do, which added together equals 12/12, simplifies to 1. Of course unless 2/12 of the girls are neutral towards boys like you, then it would be 7/12 don't, 3/12 do, 2/12 are honey badgers who don't give a fuck.
>
> -signed a math teacher

ONLINE DATING IS HELL

SIMPLE LINES FOR SIMPLE MINDS

Hi what is your favorite kind of sex?

    Good Sex

I want you

    I want me too.

What's it going to take to get your sexy little ass in my bed?

    Rohypnol

Okay so if you don't want a relationship why put on your profile you're looking for one?

    How else am I supposed to lure in my innocent victims?

ONLINE DATING IS HELL

Found anyone interesting on here?

> I haven't run across myself yet so no.

most interesting woman I've seen here…

> I should get a deal with Dos Equis

You have got to be the most beautiful woman I've ever seen

> You don't get out very often, do you

So what's your favorite position?

> Fetal

You look like trouble 😋

> You are quite astute. I am trouble.

ONLINE DATING IS HELL

Good afternoon!! I must say, you are way too beautiful to be on a dating website!!!

> Agreed. But I'm also a raging bitch from hell so it all evens out.

What's up gorgeous.

> I'm torturing men. Are you next?

Hello I'm James how are you doing tonight beautiful

> Massage therapist AND chef? Are you trying for the full gamut of panty dropping careers.

Hi. I like your smile. How do you relax after a stressful day?

> Masturbate

Sexy and pretty pics. Do those shoes come with wrist straps ;)

> No. I need quality made leather cuffs for the shit I like to do

ONLINE DATING IS HELL

So I just asked Siri what to say to this woman with a cute smile on okcupid…

> And she said "You don't have a chance"

I got a pretty decent cock pic the other day wanna see

> Not really honey

Cool any threesomes recently?

> Tons. I can't stop them. They happen all the time and I'm just bored with them. Time to move on to swingers parties and/or gangbangs

Do you ever wonder if "It's Raining Men" and "Let the Bodies hit the floor" are describing the same incident, but from drastically different viewpoints?

> Like one is from humanity on earth and the other is God playing the deity version of paintball but using people instead?

ONLINE DATING IS HELL

 I'd love to hear about your sexual exploits

    Wouldn't you rather be one?

Hi just looking at your pic the divorce cake is way cool. Are you into couples?

    I think the divorce cake indicates that I am not.

This is my actual celebratory cake from April 1st, 2016, the day my divorce was final.

ONLINE DATING IS HELL

Life's too short, eat dessert first!!

    Hi, I'm TinderHella but you may call me Dessert

Let me stuff you

    With cheese?

Greetings my lady. Are you prepared to be taken to a place called the top of the world? Where the attention and admiration you desire and deserve are waiting for you? If so all you have to do is accept Daddy's hand and allow me to lead you. lets connect and see if we cannot make some special

    How many of these do you send out in a day? Can you claim disability for the repetitive motion of copying and pasting?

Could we please chat and me I think there's a real good chance we might get along I find you very attractive and I can tell you're super smart and open-minded and maybe your very affectionate and

    and...? And...? AND WHAT?! I CAN'T STAND NOT KNOWING!

ONLINE DATING IS HELL

Without alcohol, I have no idea what to do with my hands that would be appropriate in public.

> Funny. I find that the inappropriateness usually increases with liquor consumption.

ONLINE DATING IS HELL

"SMALL" TALK

Men are so hilariously obsessed with size.

Hi how are you doing miss

You look and sound like fun...I want

Love to be deep in you. I'm 8.5 long n 6" round thick

> Good for you. *pats you on the head*

Tinderhella loves big cock?

> TinderHella is only 5'2

I don't have to put it all inside of Tinderhella

Is it true that the majority of women think that size matters?

> Yes, it is true. The size of a man's wallet does matter. The majority of women are shallow bitches.

ONLINE DATING IS HELL

Very nice. Sounds like you know what you want. Probably helps that other things are also taller too haha

> Things are not always proportional

Oh, well those unfortunate men. I guess I was blessed. Haha

Just know that I am very tall :)

> Yes. 6'4

6'4 and 10 inches. Ha

> Good for you. But giving someone a big bat doesn't mean he knows how to use it.

Hey how are you

Do you like young..large guys?

> Like fat toddlers?

I'm 12.5

> Good for you.

ONLINE DATING IS HELL

Wow ur sexy n gorgeous and sound even better enjoyed ur profile and Qn.. I'm Hank frm southern California however I am goin to be in the area the week of 11/7.. I'm all Italian stallion n 6'2.. hope to tlk wth u..

> What does that mean? Italian Stallion? Huh?

What do u think it means ?

Hows it goin

Stallions r fun to ride

> You have hooves and a tail? I have no fucking clue what you are talking about

ONLINE DATING IS HELL

DESPERATION - A NEW COLOGNE FOR MEN

Please stop bathing in it.

What do you like?

I like to fuck however she wants to be fucked. I adapt well.

So if I wanted to fuck in a vat of pudding in front of old folks in a nursing home, would you?

Yeah I would lol I don't care.

He should...

Lol was that the wrong thing to ask? "How's your weekend?" *Read deleted*

I'm not interested. Good luck in your search.

copy
paste
Repeat ad infinitum

ONLINE DATING IS HELL

8 minutes ago: Hmmm. I got home field advantage in my hotel room if u want to play

7 minutes ago: Those leggings are better than hockey skates

4 minutes ago: Well i thought i was witty

Now: I didn't make the draft?

Now: Damn

> Now: Dude. It's been 8 minutes. Chill out.

2:13am - What's up pretty lady

2:15am - So if you're up this late I'm going to take a shot into the wild and ask you if you have any sexy pictures you're down to send me ;)

2:17am - Or not, I guess I scared you away

> 2:19am - 4 minute freak out? Chill

2:19am - I'm a little hammered

ONLINE DATING IS HELL

I pissed him off somehow. Oops!

    What the fuck is your problem!

        You tell me

    You need to calm down!

Three hours later

    Can I still fuck you?

    So how about that number

    I swear I'm only a little crazy

    What is tinder hella

    And y are you so beautiful

        817-867-5309

    Score

    That's not real

    Ouch I was like excited

ONLINE DATING IS HELL

BLOCK HEADS

Different websites handle blocking others in different ways. One will delete your side of the conversation. Another deletes theirs. A third one deletes the conversation completely.

What is a "Hedonist"?

> What is "Google"?

Now why do you have to be rude?

Communication seems to be a dying thing and when I'm attempting to spark conversation of substance you reply with a condescending reply.

And youre a teacher?

SMH

Wow

> *you're

> One does not begin a meaningful conversation with demanding I be a real live dictionary.

ONLINE DATING IS HELL

Ok then. Thanks for the needless rudeness. I always loved it when a person decides to be rude instead of spending two seconds. G, I wondering if that has anything to do with your being single! Naaaah! Must be everyone else's fault.

I call this the 'hit and run' because he blocked me after making a jab at my relationship status. It's a common tactic for cowards.

This one was from the site where your side of the conversation disappears, and you get to read every insane message they sent you. I wouldn't have included it except his downward spiral is exceptionally entertaining.

> I think you are really cute and I really like your personality and I wish you would talk to me
>
> > I would [talk to you] off here but I'm hesitant to just give my number out
>
> Okay well they're not letting me send my messages they're totally censoring me
>
> Dude if it's that hard to get your number I can only imagine how difficult it must be to actually meet you in person
>
> > Dude, if you can't understand the need for a woman to be protective of her identity online, you must be a big dolt.

ONLINE DATING IS HELL

> Go ahead and Google 'dolt'. I know you haven't a clue what it means.

Omg whatever I'm here to meet people actually go out in the real world to real places not cyberspace you nerd

> *deleted*

I don't care about you identity I have a great career and better stuff to do with time than prey on your dumb identity. Wtf

> *deleted*

Dude all I was trying to do is meet you and take you out like on a date isn't that what this site is for? I told you that you were pretty and liked your personality but you tripped out on me calling a drawf or whatever idk but nevermind lady youre just an angry paranoid person

Youre ugly anyway

Thank god this 'drawf' blocked me.

ONLINE DATING IS HELL

JACKSON

Notoriously cyclists have absolutely no sense of humor*. But I made a terrible joke to one and he rightfully unmatched me. So when Jackson came along, I was much more careful. HAHAHA! I'm kidding.

You first

> I hate pretentious cyclists

> Tag, you're it

I hate hockey, and pretty much all professional franchise sports.

> Well, you're a cyclist. I don't expect you guys to have really good judgment. Even swiping right on me makes me question your ability to make sound decisions

Only one way to fix that….

> For you to quit cycling?

For me to fuck some sense into you

> You have no sense to spare. Gotta friend you'd like to volunteer? Preferably one who drives a Harley.

ONLINE DATING IS HELL

Nope

Your tits are probably bad anyway

> They are. And my ass is questionable in quality as well. Only looks good when I'm bent over something. A couch, footboard of a bed, a bar height chair, someone's lap…

I think I need to see to make sure

> All you do is keep throwing out bad idea after bad idea.

Those are the only kind I have

But whoever said you can't have a GOOD time making BAD decisions?

> I'm still not having a good time having swiped right on you

Then fucking unmatch me already! Jesus christ

For someone looking for a fun fwb you sure are a bitter bitch

XOXOXOXOXO

> Oooh, ouch. That stung

Ha! You're funny

Looking

> Damn.

ONLINE DATING IS HELL

Lighten up!

> Quit being so mean

I'm trying to be playful

Goddamnit

> Just because my vagina is numb doesn't mean my heart is. Damn, dude

I'm sorry. Friends?

….with benefits?

Lol jk

> Let's just skip the friend part

Hmmm. Alrighty

On to the naked pictures!

> I do need to add to my massive collection of dick pics. Had to buy more google drive storage to keep them all

Ha! Zing

Fuck it. That's all I got. Oh well

Ideas?

ONLINE DATING IS HELL

> How about just all out hardcore porn?

You want to make one? Yeah that's cool. Why not?

My phone takes dynamite video

> HD? Because I want to make sure you can see every blocked pore on my face, every pimple on my ass, and every ingrown hair in my crotch.

Yup yup. Top notch

> Which sleazy hotel is hosting this perv fest?

Any?

> Not just any rundown motel. Needs to have the right mix of druggies and hookers. I like to live on the edge and be naked and barefoot around used needles

Classy!

> That's actually klassy

Klassi?

> She's a stripper at Cabaret

She's my mom

> She doesn't have kids! She miscarried in the gutter

ONLINE DATING IS HELL

Wrong Klassi

> Nah, the 50-year-old covered in cigarette burns and knife scars. I can see the resemblance. Time hasn't been kind to either of you.
>
> I think she has a gunshot scar in her hip too.

You're good at this.

> That's what I've been told

We talked on and off for weeks.

Sorry about your numb vagina. Guess you'll never feel me. So sad

> I wouldn't have felt you anyway, right? So so small

Tiny

Oh well. Thanks a lot Obama

> Obama is black where it counts
>
> That even made me cringe a bit.
>
> And laugh a lot

ONLINE DATING IS HELL

Is your vagina racist?

    My vagina's grandfather was in the Ku Klux Klan

Fuck yeah Friday! Hope your racist vagina gets banged. ;)

By a bear

With sharks for arms

And an electric eel for a dick

    I did. All of that. And it was wonderful. I can barely walk today.

    What about you? Jealous of the bear?

Very

    You're hairy like one

How do YOU know?

    You have profile pictures. I have eyes.

    That I've wanted to scoop out with spoons since first seeing you

Dawwwww. I like your sweet talk. Makes me horny

    Hairy and horny? Didn't realize zoo animals had cell phones

ONLINE DATING IS HELL

This one does

> I am so smitten with you. I will never unmatch you <3

Sarcasm makes my dick hard

> And my numb vagina feel a tingle

You misspelled racist

> Quit. You're gonna make me have wet dreams

Lay a tarp down over your sheets first

> For a gutter miscarriage, you are hilarious

Xoxoxo

> Hate fucks are awesome but I've never had a "I'm so disgusted with you - you make me sick' fuck

You're missing out

> I'm sure you've had plenty where the woman suddenly realizes what she's done with her life and begins to sob.

> It isn't the massive amounts of pussy juice you're trying to keep off the mattress, it's the tears

One chick actually puked in my bed

> Are you my ex? Because I've done that

ONLINE DATING IS HELL

No

She was way hotter

>*speechless*

Finally

Awww don't be mad

I thought we were clicking

>Is someone feeding you lines? Because I know you yourself are not that good at this

Just me

Alone.

>Like every night

Yup

>I am seriously at a loss. I'm gonna have to get some ice for this burn.

>Not mad. Just proud.

?

Which burn?

ONLINE DATING IS HELL

> The hotter comment

That's probably just the syphilis

> You would know, right?

You'll live

> Good night my sweet disgusting prince. I'd totally puke in your bed too.

I'd rather have a nice long sloppy blowjob, on my dick

> I would say I could still make both happen but puke is definitely not my fetish.

No puke. Just your mouth on my cock

> I'm more of a dry hand job kind of girl

Unacceptable

> You'd be surprised at what guys will accept from a pretty girl

You know any pretty girls?

> Nope. I surround myself with trolls so I look more attractive in comparison.

How's that working out for ya?

ONLINE DATING IS HELL

    Let's hang out and we can see

Hmmm.

Idk. I think I hate you

    That makes two of us

Perfect

Hate fuck

    I hate masturbate all the time. What do I need you for?

Adios

    What does adios mean? I'm bisexual, not bilingual

It means you probably couldn't get my dick hard anyway

    Btw, I'm talking to a bodybuilder. You have 3x his IQ.

    My floppy tits and pancake ass have already come to that conclusion

Whoa

You'd probably prefer the meat head

    Nope. He kant rede

ONLINE DATING IS HELL

Dats know guud

> But I couldn't turn down a guy named Puddin.
>
> It's a weakness

You banged him already? Lol

> He was the bear. With sharks for arms. But no eel dick.
>
> It was a disappointment.

Bummer dizzle

> It's probably like touching an electrical outlet with a fork. Except I'm using my clit.

Shocking.

Jackson found me on OkCupid!

Lol

> ...goddamn it

PROFILES

When I first signed on, my profile was genuine and listed things I was looking for in a partner.

> Just having fun - important things to me - confidence and a wicked sense of humor. I like taller guys but I'm only 5'2 so everyone is taller than me. Have been described as tossable. Single after a long time of being not. Beards are good :) Baby faces belong on the babies. I tried to be shallow but turns out I like/want/need personality too. Don't waste my time if you are a bore. Low maintenance, independent, smart, hilarious, cute.

Slowly that all changed. This was my warning label. If someone still talked to me, they had essentially signed a release form.

> I am loud, brash, opinionated, passionate, inappropriate, and terrible for your mental health. I will drive you to an early grave while you tell me to rot in hell and call me a cunt. If you think you can handle this selfish, cold bitch, let's have a beer. I am a horrible person but I'm great at giving head. You may want to consult the hot/crazy scale here

ONLINE DATING IS HELL

THANKSGIVING

My extreme dislike of Thanksgiving and the concept of Black Friday led to this profile, which was the first themed profile.

> Reasons why my vagina is better than Black Friday
> 1) No need to camp out for 2 days in the freezing cold
> 2) the only pushing and shoving is when you push me on the bed and shove your cock in
> 3) more enjoyable that leftovers
> 4) a gift you give yourself, not your annoying family
> 5) truly an exclusive deal
> 6) cleaner than Wal-Mart
> 7) not limited to one per customer - if you like it, have another
> Supplies are limited so if you want to come, you best come early. And for Christ's sake, don't come without me

Guys loved them so the themes took off.

ONLINE DATING IS HELL

CHRISTMAS

This Ho Ho Ho wants you to stuff her stocking with your candy cane. You will not find her on 🎅 Santa's naughty list because she's always a nice girl. 👼

So climb down her chimney to try her cookies and see why Santa loves to come to her house every year.

ONLINE DATING IS HELL

For a few days I was asking friends and co-workers for names of Christmas songs to seek out the dirty ones.

It's the most wonderful time of the year!

O come all ye faithful and have yourself a merry little Christmas elf. It will not be a silent night if you are a good little drummer boy. The neighbors will be saying "Do you hear what I hear" when we're rockin' around the Christmas tree.

So don't be Frosty the Snowman. Be my Santa baby cuz it's cold outside and all I want for Christmas is you.

You know you want to touch my silver bells.

ONLINE DATING IS HELL

I've got a big thick candy cane ready to unload some cream on your bunny hills

---

I'll stuff your stocking so full you'll be oozing icing for days

> Oozing anything, even something as yummy as icing, isn't something I want to do for several days

---

Your little jingle reads like "welllll come bang me in a Santa costume while the elves watch"

> The elves don't watch. They listen at the door.
>
> And get the video later

Hey there, Tinderhella! I'd love to stuff my candy cane down your stocking! ;) let me know if I could cum try some of your cookies

> No.

ONLINE DATING IS HELL

You know why Santa is so jolly, right? He knows where all the naughty girls live.

> Do you think he will share that information with me? I want to know where all the naughty girls are too

---

> Hope you have a wonderful Christmas eve

Merry Christmas Eve to you too! But sorry new phone who is this again?

> No one important 😃 Enjoy your holidays!

Oh cmon don't do that!

Tinder?

I'm like 60% sure this is Tinder. Please tell me it's gonna drive me nuts

> No idea who you're talking about dude.

So that's a yes?

> How is that a yes?

Why won't you just tell me

ONLINE DATING IS HELL

I'm glad you texted me tho

> I'm enjoying the torture. Why are you glad?

Cuz I lost your number?

> And what are you going to do with it now that you have it again

Well not sure now. Kinda depends on you

> How's that?

Well if you want to see me again

> I don't know. I think I got all I needed the first time we met

Ah ha! That was a trap. Never met Tinder

> So who am I?

No idea

> You are too adorable

Ugh now I'm just confused

> We should make plans to meet and then you can see if you recognize me 😜

That sounds scary

Or maybe you should give me hints

ONLINE DATING IS HELL

> Well, you know who I am not now

Yup, one down. About 6.99 billion to go

> I am female so I cut that 7 billion in half. So really more like 3,499,999,999

Touché

> Ooo, you could just remind me what your address is and I'll show up. Could be good. Could be bad. Could be ugly.

Do I still get to slam in the door in your face

If you're not someone I want to see?

Have we actually met in person?

> I find it hard to believe all your female contacts were as sarcastic as this

Jesus Christ idk! Answer the question

> No we haven't met. I kinda gave up trying after a few times

It's Tinder, got it.

> Would you have slammed the door in my face?

Eh...probably not. My dick would have taken over

ONLINE DATING IS HELL

So what's the deal? Haven't had a good fuck in a while or just wanted me? lol

> You are my white whale.

ONLINE DATING IS HELL

NEW YEAR'S EVE

For Auld Lang Syne, my dear, I have a cup of more than just kindness for you.

I would love to ring in the new year with a new someone.

Tall, handsome men can apply to help me follow the tradition of first-footing and cross my threshold. Come in the front door and finish your good luck visit through the back.

I'm all out of black-eyed peas but your first meal of the new year could be me.

His profile: I don't really give a f*ck how tall you are. You shouldn't either.

I stopped reading after the word "tall"

> Yet you still swiped right

Likewise? As you can see I don't care about how tall you are. I don't choose my partners based on their height.

> Apparently you missed the sarcasm of the entire profile

ONLINE DATING IS HELL

Apparently so

Maybe you'll teach me some sarcasm.

> Lesson 1: You are lucky I didn't say tall, smart, and handsome. That would have been 3 strikes against you

> So how tall are you? Can I wear heels or no?

I am 5'6 but I don't mind if you wanna wear heels to be honest.

> I don't care if you mind. I've never gone out with someone where I could see the top of his head. I'm 5'2. I like heels.

I like women wearing heels too.

> Well at least you won't have to stand on your tiptoes to look me in the eye

Hit me up if you wanna see my dick pictures

> I'll add it to my massive collection of unsolicited dick pics.

> I had to get a whole hard drive to store them.

Being a woman is tough these days eh?

> Dicks dicks dicks everywhere

> And then they send me pictures of their dicks

> What's dnb?

ONLINE DATING IS HELL

Do nothing Bitch refers to the chicks relying on their men for everything

They do nothing but spread their legs

> Are you aware of how exhausting it is to spread your legs and hold back a grimace while some dumb asshole pounds into you with no care for your own pleasure? I am. That's a job in and of itself.

Lol you are missing the big picture

They are more interested in money and shit

> That flew right over your head but that isn't that hard, is it

So when are we meeting for coffee miss

> Not coffee. Paintball. Bring it.

Paintball?

Paintball is a team game bro. Can't play two people. Although I'd be super down.

> I know that! We join opposite teams and learn about each other through the art of war. We'll end up being the only 2 left because we're both so teeny

ONLINE DATING IS HELL

YOU LITTLE DEVIL

Funny but too subtle. My profile picture was of me in a blue dress and my last name was Pherr. I laughed way too hard at my own joke.

Hey! Just got back from spending the holidays in Georgia and I'm back in the area!

My name is Lucy (don't know why it says Tinder) and I'm looking for a tall, handsome fruitarian possibly named Adam. I'm in contract law and don't have time for a relationship beyond fwb so hopefully you are up to spending the night with me

Atheist so Christians should just keep swiping.

BTW, fuck the New Jersey Devils. Go Stars!

I am going to hell.

ONLINE DATING IS HELL

God created a beautiful blessing which is u

> At one time Lucifer was God's favorite and the most beautiful of all the angels. Soooo...spoiler alert!

I do prefer sluts

> Cheaper than whores

lol...only pretend dirty little whores for me. I never got the whole paying for it. I need a woman to want me, not my cash for an hour

> You are always paying for something when it comes to women. It just may not be explicitly by the hour.

Don't totally agree, but maybe

> Don't know what you got 'til it's gone.

Yeah you miss the really really dirty sluts. I find it's tougher to get them initially, after they find themselves missing one thing or three often enough.

> I was talking about your soul.

ONLINE DATING IS HELL

His profile: In an open relationship, looking for someone mature enough, and who is okay with that or has a similar situation. Drama free, educated, happy, discreet, easy going. Any questions just ask.

You also don't need to waste your time telling me why you don't agree with this lifestyle. This is Tinder, not Eharmony…

> I'm not going to tell you that your lifestyle is wrong. But have you met Jesus, our Lord and Savior?
>
> He would like to see you in his office.
>
> He sent me.
>
> Says you don't check your email.
>
> Maybe he's being sent to your spam folder? You should check on that.

> I could be the priest and you be the nun.

Cross dress…nope

> Ok, you priest, me an altar boy

Ooooo

ONLINE DATING IS HELL

I don't think so

> I know, I'm going to hell for that one

Lol...yes you are

What do you do?

> I live off alimony

Gotcha. So what's a girl who lives off alimony do on a Thursday night?

> Drink wine alone

And masturbate?

> I use a straw so I can do them at the same time

Well wine isn't my go-to but I do like it. What do you prefer?

> I lied. I actually only drink champagne and the tears of my ex-husband
>
> They both keep me looking young

ONLINE DATING IS HELL

Tell me what you're looking for?

    Anything from friends to soulmate

That's a big range

    I'm kidding. Soulmates don't exist

ONLINE DATING IS HELL

HOCKEY

The hockey profile was the most popular and the one I used the longest.

Want to win the Stanley Cup? I'm looking for a man to score through the 5 hole.

You'll get the point when you're inside my crease and you assist me with a hat trick. Slap shot too early and you'll be ejected from the game for misconduct.

Let me ride your Zamboni.

Swipe right on me. I've been told I know how to handle a stick.

ONLINE DATING IS HELL

I'm not a fan of Hockey, but I can dig the innuendos.

> "I'm not a fan of Hockey" - I don't understand these words in this order.

I guess you're a big Stars fan?

> How did you know?

Maybe the sexy Stars pic or hockey talk. Never heard it like that before. Ha

> I bring a unique experience to this app for certain

I've never seen so many hockey sexual innuendos in my life

> YAY! Wish this was a category in Guinness Book of World records

ONLINE DATING IS HELL

So, per your bio, the real question is, at what point do YOU pull the goalie?!?

> When there is a race against time to make one more point before the timer runs out. Translation: when the girl wants one more orgasm before the man blows his wad

Haha. Nice!

And how many points does Tinder usually score?!?

> It's a lame game if it's anything less than 3. Means the captain is off his game and not doing his job.
>
> Like the game against the Avalanche when the Stars would just pass and pass and pass and made very few shots on goal
>
> Sometimes it's a messy goal but a point is a point.

Hello Miss Tinder I love your hockey talk..

Have you ever played? It's very fun.. I played defense so I can definitely put you on the boards lol

[His profile picture was of him dressed in a Detroit Red Wings jersey]

> I like the juxtaposition of our profile pics. Would be a very intense game. Very physical I think

ONLINE DATING IS HELL

Yes it would. I'd have to be real aggressive in your stars attire

> Have to be ready for some hip checks if you wanna play the game, right?

Hey Tinder! How are you doing today?

I am pretty good at hockey. Wayne Gretzky is my homie

Can I lick your asshole?

> Sure, why not

> I like it a bit rough. Finesse play has its place but I definitely prefer a more physical game

Not drawing a roughing penalty but yes I agree. Pulling of some hair, choking, and spanking are fair game

> That is all good enough for me

You sound like fun

ONLINE DATING IS HELL

I see you like the Dallas Stars like I do. Are you free?

> No I'm pretty damn expensive, thankyouverymuch

I didn't mean that but ok.

> Did you mean single or did you mean busy?

Busy. But I'm pretty sure the way you came at me that you are not my type. My mistake.

> Yeah if you think that was "coming right at" you, you are probably right.

LOL quite possibly the best sports analogy ever! You dear are awesome!

> That's what I've been told.

Hey there

> America and Whataburger over In-N-Out anyday

You are very correct

> I always am

Oh is that so?

ONLINE DATING IS HELL

The real question is were you wearing anything under that stars shirt

    Nope

    See, right again

Oh really, that is so sexy

Wouldn't mind investigating what's under there

That's if you could handle it

    I probably can't

    I just can't stop being right

    Blackhawks whipped our asses tonight.

    Wish I could score as much as they did.

ONLINE DATING IS HELL

Well… Ok… Lemme see… I Benn lookin forward to findin a Lady who can keep me from Seguin cause, I guess, I've Benn Lehtonen 'em… Ok… Beyond that is just too much for me. I tried, though.

> Wow, you really are pretty Sharp.
>
> Oduya really need a woman to Kari on a conversation? Because I also Niemi a man who enjoys hockey. I don't wish to Fiddler around with Jyrki men.
>
> I too am having trouble Eakin out anymore.

I want to believe you didn't mean to put that many innuendo, it just happened naturally.

> What's an innuendo?

Let me ride your Zamboni?

> I would give almost anything to be on one of those powerful machines as it works to create that slick surface, making the rink so easy to play in. So amazing.

ONLINE DATING IS HELL

His profile: I'm here to meet new people! If you are a little crazy, lots of sass, quick wit and full of snappy comebacks and puns we will have fun!

Hockey and single? I want to invite you on a ride on my slip n slide

> Is it ok if I'm a lot crazy? Not in a 'I'll stab you in your sleep' way…

It's best that you are so we can get along! Bc I'm a lot crazy not in a 'I'll feed you in bits to your walrus' way…

Did I scare you? Coo coo ka choo?

> It's only been 2 hrs! Don't get all needy and overly attached already

ONLINE DATING IS HELL

ZACH

His profile said it seemed impossible to meet anybody outside a bar. I begged to differ.

> You meet at the grocery store. Stand by some vegetables, wait for a pretty woman to walk by, make a terrible euphemism about the cucumbers being jealous of you. Or say "is that a zucchini in my pants or am I happy to see you?" Then break down crying about how lonely you are. Grown men in touch with their feelings are really hot.
>
> You're welcome.

That zucchini is jealous of me. It's lonely.

> It's the only thing that's been in your pants in a long time, huh.

Besides my hand a minute ago

> Got to do that on occasion or it will forget what skin-to-skin contact feels like

I like to let it build up for someone else to take care of. I just tease me.

> Your balls have gone beyond blue to dark purple.

Nearly black at this point. Still smooth though.

ONLINE DATING IS HELL

> That happens when you fill water balloons up with ejaculate

Is it ejaculate if it never gets out?

> *Google* *Wikipedia* …. huh. There is a video of a man ejaculating on the Wikipedia page for ejaculation. Totally makes sense. *click*

I have no urge to see that.

> I think the entire page is an elaborate joke. But you don't have to confirm that.

Always looking for new porn.

> Did you think this morning when you woke up that you'd ever have a conversation like this before the end of the day? I know I didn't. And I have some weird-ass conversations.

I did not expect that, no. Not going to complain. It's been interesting.

Almost as interesting as your profile. One might surmise you're a hockey fan.

> I'm having a hard time looking away from that webpage. Did you know there was something call hypospermia? I don't know what it is but the word itself is awesome.

> Why would you think I was a hockey fan?

ONLINE DATING IS HELL

Idk, the paragraph long metaphor comparing hockey to your vagina=Hockey fan

Those socks are amazing regardless

> I think my profile listing how my vagina was better than Black Friday is my best. And filthiest.

Lmao. I'd read that.

Which got you more activity? The sports I bet

> I am a hockey fan.

I can be a Dallas fan as long as they aren't playing the Wings

> I matched with a red wings fan. He was an asshole. Got mad when I wouldn't meet him within 24 hrs.

Don't judge us all from one asshole! What's with the 24 HR rule. That's weird.

> I'd only give you 12. ;)

ONLINE DATING IS HELL

    Ya gotta pin the girl down before then or you get ghosted

Seems the clock is ticking on us already and I didn't even know it.

    Don't freak the fuck out on me! We'll survive this!

    Just a small hiccup in our relationship

If we can get past this we can do anything.

    Absolutely! So glad you and I are on the same page

We've got 19 hours left, easy.

    Omg! The pressure!

    Like in your balls.

Pressure! Mine and your va JJ. I know you're all worked up right now after talking about my balls for the last two hours.

    A full 2 hrs of testicle talk. My favorite.

Next time, all about your clit please. My favorite.

    We only have 18 hrs left before this all falls apart and we have to get lawyers involved. Let's get all the clit talk out...off to

ONLINE DATING IS HELL

>wikipedia to find what wild, wonderful things can be learned about it

>And I'm not disappointed.

>Did you know an ostrich has one?

That bird! That must be easier to find for me.

Wiki should be banned

>I love it more than anything else in the world right now

What else did you learn on your research?

>Do not look up with a spotted hyena uses its clitoris for. Ugh

Like I don't have to now.

Serious hormones.

>Whose hormones? Yours?

Mine, yours, female hyena's.

Hours left, haven't been ghosted yet, still hope.

>Shit. Time to start the ignore process....

I'll prepare myself for the inevitable disappointment that follows the silence.

ONLINE DATING IS HELL

> Prepare by getting all your follow-up "hey" "hi" "you there?" "Guess you aren't interested"

I've really been trying to mix it up with random motivational messages. Leave it positive!

> You have to occasionally rant like a lunatic though

> Really let them know what they'll be missing.

> Call her a few foul names.

A bunch of crazy. No way. I just hope I find you one of their friend instead. :p

I'm sorry, my mother would smack me from across the country if I didn't bow out gracefully. Must respect the women.

> All in good fun

You on the other hand can go all bat shit on some dude. Totally acceptable.

> It's expected of me

Of course. The hotter you are the crazier you get to be. So don't let me down. I'm expecting some quality crazy.

> Yes sir!

> You are aware that you didn't reply to me for a solid 8 hrs right?

ONLINE DATING IS HELL

Sorry for that whole sleep thing. And I got a massage first thing this morning. Do we tack that onto the end. Give ourselves some breathing room on that deadline?

> No. We lost that time forever. It's like you don't really care if we succeed or not.

Are you there?

Practicing.

> I WAS DRIVING YOU PSYCHO!

> See how that works?

Well played sir. I am here for your amusement.

> Like you had to say that

Right again

> I always am

Yes mistress

Zach and I actually went out a few times. Thanks Wikipedia!

ONLINE DATING IS HELL

STAR WARS

I used a picture of Leia in her skimpy slave outfit as my profile picture. So many men thought that was me. I appreciate them letting me know who the true fans were.

You: stuck up, half-witted, scruffy looking nerf herder. Me: a spirited, high ranking military officer and princess with a thing for scoundrels and tall Stormtroopers. Don't tell me you love me because I already know.

I'm looking for my own Han Solo. Gorgeous and sarcastic as fuck.

Help me, Tinder-Wan Kenobi. You're my only hope!

But, if sex is all that you love, then that's what you'll receive. I'll even show you the slave collar I got from Jabba.

PS - you better not shoot first

ONLINE DATING IS HELL

OKCUPID

I finally stepped into the world of OkCupid. You weren't losing people from swiping and could read more about the other person with the longer profiles. Both of these allowed me many more opportunities to fuck around with people.

My self-summary

> I asked some friends to describe me.
>
> "Tiny but with the courage of a bull"
>
> "Snarky, entertaining"
>
> "Twisted, intellectually sensual yet downright demented"
>
> "A c**t"

I love my best friend.

ONLINE DATING IS HELL

My profile on OkCupid said "Magnets. How do they work?" and "Message me if you know who TinderHella is."

So. Can I be completely honest with you...?

> Always

I don't know how magnets work either. I think it's some sort of magical art. Also, no idea what a tinder hella is.

Wow, feels good to get that off my chest. How is the okcupid treating you?

> Well, I've learned nothing about magnets and no one's learned about TinderHella so frankly this place is treating me like shit.

ONLINE DATING IS HELL

Q&A

OkCupid has a humongous vault of questions you can answer so you can find someone more closely matched. Some were valid. Some were poorly worded. Some were bizarre. They were all obviously written by the public. The answers were multiple choice but had a blank underneath where you could elaborate. I elaborated a lot.

Can you perform oral sex on yourself?

● No

> I cannot because I have a skeleton.

What's your relationship with marijuana?

● I smoked in the past, but no longer.

> Marijuana and I have chosen to see other people.

ONLINE DATING IS HELL

Are you attracted to dangerous situations?

● Yes

> I am a dangerous situation.

Which would you rather be? Weird or normal?

● Weird

> Who the fuck wants to be normal? And what is "normal" anyway?

What kind of party would you rather throw?

○ Cocktail
○ Kegger
○ Dry
○ Orgy

> Why not all of them?

ONLINE DATING IS HELL

Do you imagine you're louder than average (for someone your gender) during sex?

● Yes, I'm louder

> I don't imagine I'm louder. I just am. I've had people complain.

Immediately after having sex with a partner, which of the following sounds most appealing?

● Sleeping.

> If it's done right, I'll be passed out and snoring away

Do you like to dance?

● Yes

> Like nobody's watching!

> Hell, I hope nobody's watching. I don't dance well.

ONLINE DATING IS HELL

Biting?

● Yes

> If you bite like an old lady without her dentures, we have nothing to talk about.

Is a woman who's slept with 100 men a bad person?

● No

> Inherently no but I have to admit that saying 100 men when you're 20 is way different than saying 100 when you're 40.

Is a man who's slept with 100 women a bad person?

● No

> Inherently no but I have to admit that saying 100 women when you're 20 is way different than saying 100 when you're 40.

ONLINE DATING IS HELL

Could you date someone who loved you with all their heart, and whom you liked a lot, but who was terrible in bed?

● No

> Interesting wording here. Your partner loves you but you only like them a lot? Why would this be asked in this manner?

What's your deal with harder drugs (stuff beyond pot)?

○ I do drugs regularly.
○ I do drugs occasionally.
● I've done drugs in the past, but no longer.
○ I never do drugs.

> Shouldn't this say "I've never done drugs"? Because technically I never do drugs anymore either but I have in the past. I could ethically answer "I never do drugs". Just one more poorly worded question for the vault.

ONLINE DATING IS HELL

Personally, is sex in a public place hotter than indoor sex?

● No

> Another bizarrely worded question. Indoor sex can be public. Should be private/public OR indoor/outdoor.

Have you ever secretly sniffed an undergarment of someone you had a crush on but were not sexually involved with?

● No.

> I want to know who the hell is writing these questions!

ONLINE DATING IS HELL

THE EMAIL WHERE I HAVE OFFICIALLY BEEN DEEMED ATTRACTIVE

Hey TinderHella,

We detected that you're now among the most attractive people on OkCupid.

We learned this from clicks to your profile and reactions to you in Quickmatch. Did you get a new haircut or something? Well, it's working!

To celebrate, we've adjusted your OkCupid experience:

You'll see more attractive people in your results.

This won't affect your match percentages which are still based purely on your answers and desired match's answers. But we'll recommend more attractive people to you. You'll also appear more often to other attractive people.

Sign in to see your newly-shuffled matches. Have fun, and don't let this go to your head.

ONLINE DATING IS HELL

It's true! They were hiding the hot dudes! It was as if Willy Wonka had opened the door to a world of pure imagination:

> If you want to view hot new guys
> Simply look around and view them
> Anyone you want to, do him
> Want to bang these men?
> There's nothing to them

I was like a kid in a candy store and I just couldn't help myself

> It is time to get your sexy ass into my bed

Oh my. What would you let my sexy ass do to yours..

> Sorry for the frank opening line. If you see the time I wrote you, you'd understand late night and alcohol

You didn't answer my question.

> Fuck me until I forget what planet I'm on

ONLINE DATING IS HELL

I DIDN'T SEE THAT COMING

Well aren't you adorable

3 min. ago

I am. And I have a big cock

1 min. ago

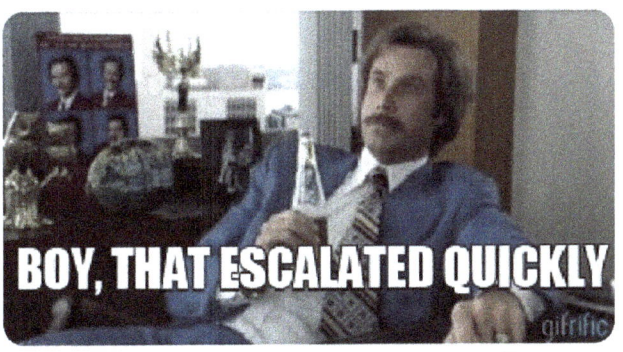

Sent

ONLINE DATING IS HELL

I will tie you up and spread your legs as wide as possible and enter you raw

Nice boobs and u look beautiful

    "nice boobs"

    swoon I'm in love!

You have nice socks

Can I try them on?

So do you wanna get some pizza and fuck?

You seem hilarious and definitely not a Trump voter!!! Lol

ONLINE DATING IS HELL

You ok with a guy licking from clit to booty?

> I'm not ok with anything

Ok

Would you suck my cock sometime?

> No.

Alright thanks for the response. I'm happy to chat or please you but have a good one otherwise.

Let's get a drink. When are you free?

> October 23, 2029 - 11:15-11:18 pm
>
> I'll pencil you in.
> Well, when we're facing each other, we're the same direction so we'll probably bump dicks.

ONLINE DATING IS HELL

> The way to this girl's heart is through Deep Eddy's lemon vodka.
>
> It's also helps get you into this girl's pants.

His profile: If your first picture is of your cat, God help you. I'm a sucker for corn rows and manicured toes

> If the first picture is of your cat, god help you....because I will ravage you senseless you foxy lady! ...right? I completed that thought correctly? Not that my first picture is of my cat. It is some fine pussy but it's not my cat.

Well hey. How's it hanging?

> Low and to the left

Interesting. I tend to hang right. Is that a problem?

ONLINE DATING IS HELL

My cock needs your cum so you can sick it off

> Sick it off? You want me to puke on your cock? That's gross, man

Oops, suck it off. "Sorry"

> And then you want me to suck the vomit off? Da fuq, dude?

Wat ever rocks your boat.

> Uh, I'm not the one in the boat and I definitely would be vomiting somewhere if I was being rocked in one. Just gross. Ugh.

Well let's get together on flat land then, lunch?

Hey there!

Do you let men lick your anus?

ONLINE DATING IS HELL

His main profile picture was him holding a box of donuts.

> Swiped right for the donuts.

U can eat donuts off my cock, if you'd like. I can hold a little over a half dozen on the donut stick! Hope that wasn't toooo forward ^_^

> That's way too much sugar for anyone. Are you going to pay for my insulin?

Sure! I'll administer the shots for you.

Where do you want it? Your ass?

> Well I usually inject myself in the thigh but the buttocks are acceptable locations too

Wait, are you really diabetic?

> No, I was just playing along.
>
> Right now I'm craving burgers. How many of those can you fit on your wing-wang

ONLINE DATING IS HELL

Hey those are some sexy socks. I'd like to see more of what's under them.

Calves and feet. Do you have a foot fetish or something?

Yes, I do. Is that a deal breaker for you? Didn't mean to speak so soon, the pic is just very sexy.

I was making a sarcastic joke. Didn't realize I hit the mark so closely 😜

Men, when posting pictures of you with different beard lengths, please let us know which one is most recent so I don't have to has questions like:

From 0 to 10, 0 being newborn baby and 10 being a grizzly bear, where is your beard growth?

I'm not a fan of billy clubs.

I thought you're into the rough stuff.

which is how I know I'm not a fan of billy clubs

ONLINE DATING IS HELL

Sometimes it escalates so much that I make myself cringe. I feel so guilty every time I laugh at this.

You're into sarcasm, right?

> No, I think mean-spirited fun is offensive

Hehe yes give me more

> Making light of people's shortcomings is a trigger for me. I was assaulted by a clown when I was younger.

That's awful. Was it your daddy or uncle?

> It was your dad. You are the biggest joke he ever made.

ONLINE DATING IS HELL

HELLA - THE REBOOT

I've deleted and restarted my Tinder account a few times. So I'd sometimes match with the same person more than once.

> Twue wuv

Hahaha I was wondering about you

> Now I'm wondering about me too.

God...You again...

> I am a masochist. What's your excuse for swiping right again?

It obviously hadn't gone well the first time.

ONLINE DATING IS HELL

HARRY POTTER

Accio my 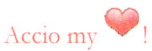!

I'm looking for a Seeker who can use his Firebolt to catch my Golden Snitch. Be my Remus in the streets and my Lupin in the sheets. My charms may engorgio your wand. Swish and flick your wand just right and your neighbors might think they live next to the Shrieking Shack.

As a Ravenclaw I value wit and intelligence.

Let's meet at the Three Broomsticks and grab a butterbeer (or Firewhisky) together.

Must be drug and Hogwarts free.

Send me pics of your chamber of secrets? ;)

Why? You want to hide your basilisk in it?

ONLINE DATING IS HELL

Very clever "About me"

I'm not into Harry Potter but I caught most of the references.

I think what makes us atheists is knowledge and having the veil pulled back from our eyes so we can see clearly. Too many people are content continuing down the path laid out by parents, never questioning. I don't swallow anything and question everything.

> I swallow a lot. Religion just isn't one of them.

ONLINE DATING IS HELL

GAME NIGHT AT HELLA'S HOUSE

hey...like to have fun ?

> Of course! Who doesn't?!?

what kind of fun u think i am talking about ?

> You just asked about "fun". I figured the only other option was "boring". And isn't something I like at all.

like to have drinks with me tonight and later some fun ? only both of us ?

> Sure! Let's drink and play all night

where do we meet and what time ?

> I don't know. Where can we order some chocolate milk and have enough table space to set up Settlers of Catan? I bet you have wood for sheep 😂

lol...hope you are joking ;)

> Joking? You asked if I wanted to get drinks and have fun. Chocolate milk is a refreshing drink that has the right sweetness without being laden with calories and Settlers is a great game.

ONLINE DATING IS HELL

lol...u r just great...i like u sorry but i was talking about something..i think u got what I was saying

> I'm busy tonight. I don't drink alcohol. I think asking someone if they like to have fun, whether it's innocent or dirty minded, is a dumb thing to ask. Do I like to have fun? No. I like to sit at my dining room table drinking tap water and eating saltines while I pay bills.

so u r not interested ? this is like once in a while… to strangers having fun… let me know if you change your mind.

> I'm going to assume you meant to say "So, you are not interested? This is like once in a while (did you mean lifetime?)...two strangers having fun...let me know if you change your mind."
>
> Points for getting the correct version of the word "your" there at the end. Still in the red though and I'm good. Thanks.

ONLINE DATING IS HELL

> I think you'll need to define 'good girl' for me. Because I don't think I'm it.

You know good girl, likes to get a bit wild and take her clothes off, likes to give head and fucked in different positions

> A good girl follows directions

Then are you a good girl

> I'm horrible at following directions. I'm mouthy, opinionated, and loud. I'm a self-centered attention whore

You can be all those things. As long as you bring that energy to the bedroom.

> Oh, don't encourage me. You might regret it.

I don't think I would.

> Maybe then we can get drinks tomorrow night? I'll bring my first aid kit.

ONLINE DATING IS HELL

Can I pull your hair?

> Can I pull your beard?

Absolutely

When

7 hours later...

Tinder game weak

> Let's go with that. My game is weak, says the guy with one picture, no face showing, and a 4 word profile.

> Back to the beard...is she hot? Because I'm bisexual.

> Really?

Well, more on the gentle side.

> Don't go gentle on me but you may want to have your guard waaaay up

> How are your reflexes

Pretty solid when randy.

> Challenge accepted.

ONLINE DATING IS HELL

I AM THAT FRIEND

I feel sorry for them

> I am hilarious.

sometimes

> Always

mmm okay whatever you say

> In my head I'm always hilarious

> I'm laughing all the time in there

ONLINE DATING IS HELL

> Not getting married at all!
>
> Ever!
>
> Ever!
>
> Fuck that shit

Ha! Well it doesn't have to be exactly like the movie.. 😊

> It won't be. He'll have to tackle me, beat me in battle, and survive me. Even then, we're not getting married.
>
> Ever.

This last one might explain my single status a bit.

EPILOGUE

Jackson is Reborn

Some of these conversations are two years old, and while I was typing them up I felt nostalgic at times. I still have many phone numbers saved and that includes Jackson's. So when I was transposing our epic back and forth, I decided to text him.

> I'm actually writing a book about my crazy antics with online dating. So I was thinking of you along with the millions of other dudes.

Glad I could contribute. Was nice to hear from you

> Have a great rest of your day!

Ditto, life even

> I wouldn't wish you any less

ONLINE DATING IS HELL

One Week Later…

So do you wanna bang my girlfriend and I?

> Picture of the gf?

You first

> I don't have a picture of your girlfriend to send you
>
> Yet.

ABOUT TINDERHELLA

Currently 41 and divorced with a couple of great kids, a plethora of great friends, and fortunately only one jackass ex-husband. I also have one cat who annoys the piss out of me.

I've retired from online dating and while I still have a Tinder account, I don't know if I'll ever return to it ever again. My looks, sense of humour, and intelligence, however, will never be shelved and I am still a thorn in the sides of my family and friends.

HellaMean.com
TinderHella.com

ONLINE DATING IS HELL

ONLINE DATING IS HELL

funny
droll
amusing
humorous
witty
jocular
silly
slapstick
zany
uproarious
ludicrous
whimsical
knee-slapping
cartoony
off the wall

ONLINE DATING IS HELL

www.ingramcontent.com/pod-product-compliance
Lightning Source LLC
Chambersburg PA
CBHW070431010526
44118CB00014B/1993